Chicken Soup for the Soul.

Miraculous Messages of Love from Beyond

Amy Newmark

CSS

Chicken Soup for the Soul, LLC
Cos Cob, CT

P9-AOU-563

Miraculous Messages of Love from Beyond
Amy Newmark

Published by Chicken Soup for the Soul, LLC www.chickensoup.com

Copyright © 2019 by Chicken Soup for the Soul, LLC. All Rights Reserved.

The publisher gratefully acknowledges the many publishers and individuals who granted Chicken Soup for the Soul permission to reprint the cited material.

Front cover photo courtesy of iStockPhoto.com/ jack-sooksan (© jack-sooksan). Interior photo courtesy of iStockPhoto.com/ Irochka_T (© Irochka_T).

Cover and Interior by Daniel Zaccari

ISBN: 978-1-61159-707-3

PRINTED IN THE UNITED STATES OF AMERICA
on acid∞free paper

25 24 23 22 21 20 19   01 02 03 04 05 06 07 08 09 10 11

Table of Contents

Miracle of the Green Tide

*When you open your mind to the impossible,
sometimes you find the truth.*
~From the television show *Fringe*

I'm a nurse. I always believed in science, not miracles. That is, until I experienced one of my own.

It happened one August day, walking the shoreline from Red Rock in Swampscott, Massachusetts, to the Tides, a restaurant in nearby Nahant. I had done this nearly every day that summer. But that day, dismal and gray, was different, sadder, for it marked the tenth anniversary of Dad's fatal stroke. With each step, I relived that pain.

Back then, I'd just returned home from errands and casually hit the answering machine. "Your dad has been rushed to Springfield Hospital. We found him on the floor." It was a neighbor of his. "I think he had a stroke."

I grabbed some things for the two-and-a-half-hour drive. Mom was away visiting family in Charleston, South Carolina. My brother lived in Texas, my sister in Myrtle Beach.

Dad, a vibrant seventy-eight-year-old, walked and played golf almost daily. He did all his household chores and was repairing the porch roof. Months earlier, he had cheered as I graduated as a nurse practitioner.

When I saw Dad, I knew it was not good. He had suffered a massive stroke, his entire right side paralyzed. He could not sit, speak, nor swallow. But he was alive and his eyes showed relief—his daughter, his nurse, had arrived.

Luckily, he understood me. "Daddy, you're going

to be okay," I repeated, trying to hide the fear in my eyes. I phoned my mother and siblings. That night, and for most of the next fourteen, I stayed by his side.

Dad could not tell me what he wanted or needed, frustrating us both. Then, I gave him a pad and put a pen in his left hand. He scratched out a few words. Dad was still there.

Dad was so ill that he could not make his own health care decisions. The doctor explained that he needed a "health care proxy," to authorize someone to make health care decisions. "Dad, who should this be?" Slowly but clearly, he wrote, "Bonnie (my childhood nickname) is in charge."

Over the next few days, Dad seemed to improve, and that weekend, he rallied. With support, he sat up to enjoy time with his wife, children, and grandchildren. As we were leaving for dinner, he teasingly wrote, "Make sure Dick (my brother) picks up the check!" Dad always had a fondness for greenbacks. Surely he must be getting better, I thought, if he's thinking about money!

Dad still could neither eat nor swallow. A tube in his nose was giving him liquid nutrition, but it was only temporary. Now we had to decide if a permanent tube should be put in his stomach. Would Dad want that? I recalled our talks about his wishes. I carefully weighed the benefits and risks of such a procedure. My mom, brother, and I were uneasy about it. But my sister in Myrtle Beach insisted, "You just can't starve him to death!"

In the end, Dad went to the OR. After many long hours, he was rolled back on a stretcher, a permanent feeding tube in this abdomen. I looked at his face, the pain visible. His eyes spoke, "Why did you let them do this to me?" I was shaken. Had I let Dad down?

The next day, his condition worsened. He was burning with fever and was not responding to my voice. He could not sit, write, or communicate in any way. The antibiotics were ineffective. A brain scan confirmed that he'd suffered another, more severe stroke, with irreversible brain herniation causing all basic life functions to quickly fail. There was nothing more that could be done, the doctor said.

I thought about my grandmother. Dad had found her collapsed from a stroke. She died within weeks. Dad said it was "for the best;" she wouldn't have wanted to live "like that" completely dependent on others. Neither would he, he said.

I recalled our talks about the difficult end-of-life decisions made by my patients and their families. He'd listened, then had nonchalantly said, "When my time comes, you'll know best what to do for me." Nothing was ever written. It was understood then. It was understood now.

Being a devout Catholic, Mom consulted the priest, then calmly said, "We can't let Dad continue to suffer. We have to let him go in peace."

Dad's care now changed from curing to care, comfort, and dignity. The antibiotics and tube feedings, no longer helpful, were stopped. His only medications were for comfort. This decision was too excruciating for my sister in Myrtle Beach, who shrieked, "Who do you think you are, Dr. Kevorkian?"

But Dad was our focus. In his final journey, we chose the path of least suffering. He'd been there for me at my birth and I would be with him in his death.

We all had our final goodbyes. In the end, he left on his terms, in a brief peaceful moment, with Mom, his love, at his side.

Now, ten years later, I walked the shoreline recalling my sister's words and the anguish in Dad's face when he returned from the OR. Had I let Dad down? I softly sobbed.

All that summer, I'd walked the beach finding treasures: starfish, shells, sand dollars, a green bottle, an unopened green can of beer, and green sea glass. I even found a denture with inlaid gold initials, but never any money. So, being my father's daughter, I thought, Dad, if I did the right thing, please send me a sign? Let me find some real money!

Just then, sloshing through the area called the Red

Tide (really harmless red algae) I looked down—a green one-dollar bill! "Wow!" I chuckled. "But gee Dad, couldn't you do better? More like a $100?"

No sooner had I giggled, there it was, another green bill! I reached down; it was a $100 bill! Oh my God! This couldn't be real! Was it a fluke or was it the sign that I'd been seeking?

I shook my head in disbelief. Could a ship have sunk in the harbor? Not feasible. Could someone have lost his wallet in the surf? Not likely. Could someone have been robbed? Nothing about it in the paper.

I need to find one more dollar to prove this was real. I had to prove this was not just some strange coincidence. So I searched, turning over red algae; not another dollar appeared. I drove home stunned. Who finds $100 on the beach?

The next day, I walked the same shoreline, puzzled and uncertain. Then, as I passed through that red algae, there it was—another dollar!

This was no coincidence, I knew then. The red

tide had turned to green money, a sign from Dad that I had not let him down. From that moment, I felt at peace.

I still believe in science. I'm still skeptical about many things. I still think of my father and miss him. But now I am a nurse who believes in miracles.

—Barbara A. Poremba—

A Simple Answer

Angels descending, bring from above,
Echoes of mercy, whispers of love.
~Fanny J. Crosby

I walk the beach, the moist sand feeling rubbery on my feet. Occasionally I must stop to wipe away a small pebble stuck on a toe or heel. A small reminder my physical body feels pain also.

It is the in-between season now, not summer with the swimmers and the families on the beach. Not yet winter, when the cold wind from Lake Michigan makes this walk almost impossible. My body is bundled, but my toes are bare in the sand.

My life for so long was an in-between. Some

days wanting to stay with him, some days frustration making me consider leaving. Thirty-eight years of marriage is a long, long time, like old ruts in a dirt road you drive on. Bumpy with age and worn in spots, making part of the drive miserable, but part of it smooth, a pleasure. Worn old patterns we fell into, him first, then me. Maybe it was the other way around. Hard to know, and I tell myself it doesn't truly matter anymore who's angry and who's not.

Not that I can't go to anger, because I can. It takes a second to send me back to one of our memories, a fight or more likely a non-fight, words never said, never truly expressed. I say them now, "Why couldn't you? Why didn't you?"

Can you fight with a ghost? Are all our old words now irrelevant? Unresolved? Like taking a sword and jabbing at a windmill. What sense does anger make in grief?

No in-between for him and me anymore. Now it is just me—me with my future, with my decisions—me alone. The long debate: am I happy, am

I not? Do we work, do we not? It is gone from my will. Off the table more quickly than I could ever have believed possible. Taken and shelved away. I try to focus my eyes forward, looking only for me. Hoping and praying the good parts of life remain for him in spirit, for me on earth.

It is my birthday today. For him, my birthday was always simple, a card that said love with a $100 bill inside for me to spend. My daughters and grandchildren over for a dinner I would make, wine to drink, small noses to play with, the little ones on my lap. Life we created and made, the two of us, then the four of us, extending now beyond our nucleus. Afterwards I would gripe to myself about the mess to clean up as all of them scattered back to their lives, leaving me once more to be the mistress of the kitchen.

This birthday feels so different, as they all will from now on. I'm at my sister's house celebrating a new way, in an old form.

"Like when we were kids," she told me when

she called to offer the stay. "Been a while since we've done this," she had added, trying to put cheer in her voice. Millions of years back I think, a different time, a different family. And so I came to try on the new, forcing myself forward in my new role as widow on my birthday.

"Guide me," I request of him, my newly departed husband, as I continue my walk. "Protect me when you can, send me hints of where to go, who to trust." Would he do that for me? But such a thought goes away quickly. I know the answer. Even in life I would know this answer.

"Of course," he would say, dismissing the question, turning his attention back to his book, his evening football or baseball game. It would be a given for him, even without the request.

I pick up stones from the beach and cast them out in the water. I would love to skip rocks, but the water is too rough, and I have to settle for trying to hit a white cap before it disappears. A freighter passes by, chugging along the horizon, moving quickly into my life and then out. I watch it disappear on the water line, hazy at first and then gone.

I search for more things of interest using my toes as a tool to shift through the sand. They fumble along feeling something foreign, something not of the beach. I look down to discover a greenish paper. A dollar I think. Excited, I reach for it and clear the beach sand away, getting small damp grains on my fingers. Pulling the money free I brush away the remainder of the sand, ready to push the bill down into the front pocket of my jeans. I stop; I stare. The president isn't right for a dollar. I bring the bill to eye level. Tears well up in my eyes, blurring the picture, the numbers. But I've seen it; I know what it is.

"How'd you do that?" I ask, lifting my eyes to the sky, laughing and crying. I hold the hundred-dollar bill to my heart, pressing it close with both of my hands. I stand alone on the quiet beach, me and the gift, amazed and grateful.

"Come on, come on," I hear my sister's voice in

the distance. "Time to start celebrating your birthday!"

I see her jogging towards me, her hands in the air calling me back, now doing the silly jumping thing she did when we were kids.

"Time to start..." I repeat, gazing once more to the sky. I move the bill into my front pocket and smile. For him it was always that simple.

—Diana Creel Elarde—

Listening to Our Angels

If you can't hear the angels,
try quieting the static of worry.
~Terri Guillemets

Driving home after a long day of teaching computer class to a group of people, my mind whirled with ideas for the next class. The car was on "auto pilot" as I drove the familiar route home. With the windows slightly open, I could feel the warm breeze on my face and I enjoyed the sweet smell of springtime air. The large knobby tires of my Jeep Cherokee hummed along the pavement as country music played on the radio. The sound was almost hypnotic and I continued my thoughts on fine-tuning the Office

2003 class. As a new instructor, I wanted to make sure to teach people the essentials to make their work easier, without overwhelming them and putting them into a computer coma. Teaching was not easy for me. I felt uncomfortable in front of the class, even though I knew the material in depth. The major benefit was that it allowed me to work part-time so I could be there for my kids. They were, and still are, my main priority in life.

As the yellow lines of the Veterans Expressway streaked by, my mind wandered from the computer class to what I needed to get from the grocery store. What would be quick and easy to prepare? The girls had karate, so it couldn't be too heavy. I continued making the mental list as I slowed to the stoplight.

Grocery store, dinner, karate, homework… why was I still sitting at this red light? It seemed awfully long. Anxiously waiting for the light to turn, my foot was ready to release the brake and press the gas at the first sign of green.

The light turned green and my thoughts were

suddenly interrupted by the appearance of my grandmother sitting in the passenger seat next to me. She said very clearly, "Wait, just wait." I remember her holding up her left hand telling me to stop. "Don't go. Don't release that brake."

The only car in sight was a silver car behind me. I still saw my grandmother's hand telling me to wait. My foot was frozen on the brake. My mind was trying to process what was happening when a car speeding down the road in front of me ran the red light.

If I had pressed the gas when the light first turned green, as I would normally do, that car would have crashed into the driver's side door of my car. At the high rate of speed that person was driving, there is no doubt in my mind that I would not be here today if I hadn't listened to my grandmother. I glanced in my rear view mirror as if to ask, "Did you see that?" The driver behind me had wide eyes as he nodded his head, confirming that he saw the car run the light, too. I don't know if he saw my grandmother next to me, but he knew what would have happened to me, and perhaps him too, if I had pressed the gas pedal when our light turned green.

The Bible is full of stories of angels appearing. In Psalm 91:11 "For He will order His angels to protect you wherever you go." In Hebrews 1:14 "Therefore, angels are only servants—spirits sent to care for people who will inherit salvation." When it actually happens, it is hard to comprehend. My hands were shaking as I gripped the steering wheel. I cried all the way home, my mind whirling with "what ifs" and trying to understand how my grandmother came to me. Needless to say, I didn't make it to the grocery store.

I didn't tell anyone about the experience for a long time. I had to process what happened before I could share it with anyone. I remember the first time telling my family. We were in the Outer Banks of North Carolina, sitting on the porch talking and the subject of angels came up. "Grandma Wilson is my angel," I said. My heart was racing as I told them what happened. I don't know if they believed me or not. Someone made a joke and we changed the subject. Later that evening, my sister-in-law shared a story with me about her own incident with an angel. I felt such relief in knowing I wasn't the only one who had been through this. Over the years, I have shared this experience, and each time, I learn of similar encounters.

My grandmother had passed away in 1989, a year before my first daughter was born. This event occurred thirteen years later. I find comfort in knowing that she is still with us and able to see all three of my children.

I am so thankful for many things that occurred that day—to God for sending my grandmother to me, my grandmother for saving my life, and to myself for actually listening and not ignoring the warning. Our daily lives can get so hectic that we ignore the messages we receive.

—Karen McBride—

Dancing in Heaven

Dancing faces you towards Heaven,
whichever direction you turn.
~Terri Guillemets

Shortly after crossing the state line from Georgia into Alabama, I saw a handsome young man right outside my front windshield. I blinked a couple of times to focus, trying not to get too distracted from the highway I was negotiating at eighty miles per hour. But sure enough, there was Daddy, who had died twelve years earlier, his arms outstretched, grinning from ear to ear, looking off in the distance, eyes twinkling. He was thin like I remembered him when I was a little girl. Gone were the bags under his eyes and the slightly protruding abdomen. No longer was there any gray to be found on his full head of hair.

Out of the clouds on the left side of my view, a beautiful young woman came running toward him, her long wavy dark hair flowing all around her. He wrapped his arms around her.

"Oh, Huck, you are so beautiful," he whispered softly in her ear as they embraced. "Oh, David, you too," she whispered back, snuggling comfortably into his strong arms. "I've missed you so much."

"Come on, I have a lot to show you," he said, excitement in his voice. He twirled her around as if in a dance. She hesitated. "But what about the children?" she asked. In a reassuring yet insistent voice, he said, "Don't worry, they'll be fine. Janie will be there soon; they have each other. They'll be fine."

They danced off into the puffy clouds hand in hand. I wanted to remember all the details of this incredible image so I could describe it to Mama and my sisters and brother when I reached Tuscaloosa.

They'd get a big kick out of it.

Just moments before this vision, I had given up trying to find something interesting to listen to on the radio. I figured I'd just think about something else to occupy myself on the long drive from Macon, Georgia, to Tuscaloosa. As I was sorting through my brain for what I wanted to think about, Daddy had appeared.

The ringing cell phone startled me.

"Janie, pull over a minute. I want to talk to you about your mama." Why was my sister's friend calling me? How did he get my number and how did he know I was in the car? That was the only time I ever used this old-fashioned bag phone. I had yet to join the modern world of the smaller, handheld cell phones. Waiting for me to stop the car, he asked where I was and how the trip was going. I wondered why he cared. By the time I pulled off Interstate 20 onto the shoulder a few miles west of the Oxford/Anniston exit, it hit me. Something must have happened to Mama.

Shortly before I left Macon a couple of hours earlier, I told my sister, who was in the hospital room with Mama, to call me if anything changed. I was on my way to help hold a bedside vigil until Mama returned to consciousness. She had been unresponsive for nearly thirty hours. But she wasn't supposed to die. Since her heart attack six months earlier and her stroke a few days later, we had almost lost her several times. But her strong will to live always kicked in (with a lot of help from activated prayer chains), and she came back from those near-death experiences stronger and more determined than ever to get her life back.

Not this time.

The friend on the phone described the last few minutes that he and my sister held Mama's hands from each side of her bed, reciting the twenty-third Psalm—"Yea, though I walk through the valley of the shadow of death, I will fear no evil..."—and whispered comforting words to her. I closed my eyes, feeling like my own heart would stop. I pictured the monitor over her bed showing the ever-increasing space between her heartbeats, until there was nothing but silence. I could hardly breathe.

"She quietly slipped away at 3:48," he said. I glanced at the clock on the dash. Oh my gosh. That was the exact time I watched my parents embrace. I smiled through my tears, and said a quiet "thank you" to them for that gift.

I quickly got back on the road as soon as we hung up. I still had more than 100 miles to go and wanted to see Mama before the hospital staff removed her body. My sister promised to do what she could to keep Mama there, but was concerned about me driving. She didn't have to worry.

Mama kept me company, painting a gorgeous canvas for the entire world to see. I drove into the most magnificent sunset I've ever seen. And it stayed with me the entire trip, getting more dazzling every time I crested a hill. There were a few times I thought I saw Mama dancing through the clouds, splashing a little more pink here, a dab of gold there, a brilliant blue in between.

I later discovered that a few days earlier, just hours before Mama was transported for her last time from the nursing home where she was recovering to the same hospital where I was born nearly fifty-two years before, she told my other sister that she wanted to dance. At that time, we still thought that she was getting better. She had a little bit of movement in her left hand, which had been paralyzed since her stroke, and it was just a matter of time before she was coming home.

My sister picked up her limp arm and Mama started moving her good hand to the music. Of course, she was too weak to actually get of the bed and make any movements. But she was dancing with her hand. Her spirits were high—she seemed so free and wanting to just dance and play. A few hours after that, Mama took a turn for the worse and announced that she was dying—the first time she had said that in the months she had been bed-bound, despite the many crises and close calls she had survived.

She slipped into a deep coma from the morphine the nurses gave her to relieve the pains in her chest and never woke up. My brother called me that Tuesday morning and said Mama had not come out from under the morphine yet, although it was well past time for her to come around. I was driving over from Macon to help keep her bedside vigil until she woke up, which we were sure would be any minute.

But instead of waking up, she slipped away from us that afternoon and went off dancing with Daddy in the clouds, leaving her broken body behind for good. She finally got her wish to dance once more. This time, she was again in the arms of her husband of forty-two years and the father of their four children, just like the night they met.

—Jane Self—

Unexpected Help

I sought my soul, but my soul I could not see.
I sought my God, but my God eluded me.
I sought my brother and I found all three.
~Author Unknown

I sped down the interstate, my heart pounding in my chest, tears threatening to blur my vision. The call from Saint Elizabeth's, the assisted living center where my parents lived, had sent me into a panic.

"Your dad isn't doing too well. He has slumped to one side and isn't talking or eating. We'd like to send him to the hospital," said the kind voice on the other end of the line.

One thing my dad had been very clear about

after his recent bout with pneumonia was that he did not want to go back to the hospital again. He was still under hospice care, although he had made a remarkable recovery, beyond what anyone expected.

"No, please don't send him to the hospital. He is on hospice and has requested not to go the hospital. Please. I am coming. I will be there as soon as I can," I pleaded.

It was nearly an hour drive from my home in rural Boulder County to the heart of Denver where my parents lived, where I had been raised, and my parents before me. We were so glad to have found a well-kept, caring place for my parents when my mother's Alzheimer's became too much for my father to care for at home. Once in a place where my mother was taken care of, the toll of caregiving on my father became more evident. After the pneumonia, he was diagnosed with vascular dementia, caused by a series of mini strokes that left him more disoriented and debilitated each time.

"I'm coming, Daddy, please don't die, please don't die. I'm coming as fast as I can." I wished for someone else to be able to get there to help my father. My thoughts moved to my brother, who had lived closer. My brother who had been there to help me take care of my parents in previous times of need. My brother who had overdosed on drugs last month. "How could you leave me like that? Where the hell are you now, when I need you so much? When Dad needs you?"

I heard a deep, gentle and so familiar voice speak in my heart. "I am right here with you. And honey, you really need to slow down. You are driving way too fast. He isn't going to die today. Please, please slow down."

I looked at my speedometer and was shocked to see it was over ninety. I let off the gas, but my anger did not abate. "Well, why aren't you with Dad? He needs you more than I do right now. Please go to him!"

The answer was swift. "I am with him. And he is going to be okay. I can be with both of you. Pretty cool, huh?"

Tears were fully running down my face now as the brother who I missed so much, despite my anger with him, gently supported me as I dealt with my loss.

"I don't understand. Where are you, Matt? Why did you go? What happened?"

"That's a lot of questions and I think you better focus on your driving right now. Just know that you are not alone. I'm here and I'm helping you take care of Mom and Dad."

"You are not alone," echoed in my mind and I felt calmer. I drove safely to Saint Elizabeth's where my dad was already doing much better, sitting up and talking, though still disoriented. I kissed the top of his head and held his hand, grateful to be able to be there with him when he needed me. "He is not going to die today," Matt had said. And he didn't. My head was full of questions and doubt about what happened while I was driving. But my heart was full of love, for both the father beside me and the brother who had protected us that day.

—Lisa Shearer Cooper—

The Very Long Distance Call

*The most beautiful thing we can
experience is the mysterious.*
~Albert Einstein

I loved my cousin Morgan. He was, during my youth, more like an older brother to me. My love of sports, entertainment, music, etc. was heavily influenced by him. We remained extremely close into adulthood. Morgan was someone who had an almost supernatural "life force" about him. When you were in his company, you felt his vibrancy, his positivity and his goodness. I don't know how else to describe it, but anyone who met him would know what I mean. That's why it was especially devastating and shocking beyond belief that a life force like Morgan's could be extinguished, at age sixty-two, by pancreatic cancer.

There are certain people who I find it hard to believe are no longer with us. It's a strange and eclectic list, I know. It's celebrities like Dana Reeve (Christopher Reeve's wife), Tim Russert, Phil Rizzuto, Michael Jackson, Merv Griffin, Bobby Murcer, Elizabeth Edwards... just that life force thing, I guess. Morgan was in that category.

One day, about a year or so after his passing, my wife Dana and I got home early on a Saturday evening to hear a message on our answering machine. It was from Morgan's son, Adam, telling us to make sure we watched psychic John Edward's television show that evening. The program was about to start. We turned on the TV and there was Morgan's wife, Jennifer, along with their two adult children, Adam and Alana, having a psychic reading by Edward regarding Morgan's attempt to communicate with them from the great beyond.

It was pretty intense and incredible stuff. Normally I would be highly skeptical, but the ultimate shocker for Dana and I came when Edward stated that Morgan was communicating about "a certain song from the Broadway musical *Wicked*." Jennifer, Adam and Alana shook their heads, not immediately recalling any particular association between Morgan and a song from *Wicked*. But Dana and I sure knew of one.

The previous year, when it had become clear that Morgan had no more than a few days left to live, Dana handpicked a song that she felt best expressed her feelings about him. She recorded her version of the song "For Good" from the show *Wicked*, and overnighted a CD to the hospice where Morgan spent his final days. Jennifer played the song for Morgan that next evening. According to Jennifer, a very weakened Morgan smiled and cried at the recording's conclusion. And the very next morning, he passed away.

So you can only imagine how stunned Dana and I were to hear Edward mention, of all things, "a certain song from the Broadway musical *Wicked*. Nobody outside of me, Dana, and Morgan's immediate family would even know that it was the final song Morgan had listened to before he passed!

As Dana and I struggled to keep it together during the fascinating and chillingly on-target reading, the telephone rang. I hurriedly picked up the phone. There was no voice on the other end, just a loud, piercing, electronic screeching sound. Very strange, I thought, and hung up. Again the phone rang. Again that screeching sound. I don't ever remember hearing a noise quite like that coming through a phone. I hung up once more.

Even more bizarre, when I picked up the phone again I couldn't get a dial tone—just that strange electronic piercing noise, louder than ever! I checked all the connections. Everything was fine. But no matter what I tried to do, I could not get rid of that noise. Then literally within seconds of Edward's segment with Morgan's family ending, the screeching sound stopped and the dial tone mysteriously returned!

I have since been told by people who have studied the field of parapsychology that departed family members often use modern electronics to communicate from the great beyond, and that the telephone is the tool most frequently employed. No one would have found that kind of stuff more absurd than I, trust me. But Morgan, I truly believe with all my heart that it was you trying to reach us that Saturday night. And you sure did, Cuz. You sure did.

—Gary Stein—

Lilacs and Roses

Flowers seem intended for the solace of
ordinary humanity.
~John Ruskin

Grandma Ellen was dying. I knew it. Cancer was winning the battle. I was devastated that I couldn't see her, even for a few minutes, but my grandfather insisted that he wanted all the grandchildren to remember Grandma healthy and happy.

I was ten at the time and very close to Grandma. She babysat me often, so we spent a lot of time together. The hours would seem like minutes. I have many memories of us working together in the garden or the house, taking bike rides, visiting people, running errands, making meals, playing card and board games, and even napping together. I loved how she'd rub my back while we took turns spelling words aloud until one or both of us dozed off.

One night I drifted off to sleep and dreamed of Grandma. I was in the big orange seat on the back of her bike—one that I had been on frequently as a small child. She pedaled us down the paved country road to the enormous stand of lilac trees a short distance from her house. It was a place that we visited every spring when the blossoms opened. I loved how the scent of flowers intensified as we got closer, luring us forward. The sun felt so warm. The hum of bees was audible even before we got off the bike to smell, touch, and pick a big bouquet of lilacs. I woke up before we could take the bouquet back to her house. Several times that night, I had the very same dream, waking each time at that same point. Over and over it happened. I just couldn't fall into a peaceful, dreamless sleep.

Then, during one of the awake moments, I sensed someone enter my room. Lying on my stomach, I turned sleepy eyes to the closed door. Suddenly, I smelled lilacs. My bed creaked and lowered like someone was sitting down on the edge. I felt a hand upon my back, rubbing it just like Grandma always did when we napped together. In no time, I dropped into a deep, dreamless sleep.

My alarm clock woke me. A peculiar emptiness ached in my gut. I lingered in bed, remembering what had happened, clinging to those precious moments with Grandma. Something in me sensed she was gone. Eventually, I forced myself out of bed and went upstairs. My teary-eyed mother met me at the door. She gave me a long hug and in a strangled voice told me Grandma had passed away early that morning.

The news confirmed what I instinctively knew. "I know," I admitted, tears spilling while I explained that Grandma had come by to tell me goodbye since I hadn't been able to go to her.

The scent of flowers touched me one more time shortly after Grandma's death. It happened on one of the visits my mom and I made to her grave.

It was a temperate, late spring day. I knelt down on the sun-warmed earth and with my finger traced the roses engraved on her headstone.

I wondered why the stone didn't have lilacs engraved on it so I asked Mom, "Why did all of you pick roses for the stone?"

"Roses were her favorite flowers," she answered. "Grandma loved roses of all kinds. They're my favorite too."

"I thought she liked lilacs," I said. "We always picked lilacs together."

"She did like them, but roses were her favorite. She knew you preferred lilacs though. That's why she would take you to the big grove to pick them."

My throat tightened. Lilacs were my preferred flower. Grandma must have chosen that scent for me the night she said goodbye.

After a few minutes of silence, we walked back to

the car. We got in and Mom started the engine. The strong scent of roses suddenly filled the vehicle. In disbelief, I turned to Mom. She looked as stunned as I felt.

"Do you smell roses?" I asked in a choked voice.

She nodded, her eyes wide and damp.

"They were her favorite, and yours?" I asked for confirmation.

Mom nodded again and smiled. It was a sad, yet joyful smile.

The intense fragrance lasted most of the way home as we cried, laughed, and shared precious memories of Grandma Ellen. Perhaps the scents were a gift from her, or perhaps, they were simply a hint of the sweet perfume of heaven.

—Jennifer Taylor—

The Miracle Lady

Reason is our soul's left hand, Faith her right.
~John Donne

My mother and I always had a close relationship, but we saw life differently—until she was seventy-nine years old. Her faith was deep, but based on strict rules. A first-generation Italian-American, she was a creative first grade teacher with a zest for life. Used to dealing with six-year-olds, she enjoyed being in charge. My parents had a happy marriage because her fun-loving bossiness balanced perfectly with my father's kind and gentle Pennsylvania Dutch personality.

I was an idealistic child of the New Age, writing

poetry and fascinated with yoga. I knew my mother loved me and was proud of my accomplishments, but she didn't share my belief that there is more to life than what we can see and hear.

My beloved father, a high school teacher and professional musician, who said he felt closer to God in his garden than in church, died before my twenty-first birthday. At the age of fifty-four, my tough, strong mother was suddenly vulnerable and frightened. Eventually she regained her courage and returned to teaching full-time.

At age thirty-nine, living with my husband and working in Manhattan, I was hit with the news that I had breast cancer. After a diagnosis of cancer, life is never the same. Fortunately, the cancer hadn't spread, but I needed surgery and radiation. Mom insisted on taking the bus to New York to visit me after my operation. When I saw her from my hospital window, striding down the street in her red coat, I knew everything would be fine.

Cancer caused me to reflect on my life and

feelings even more deeply. I joined a dream-sharing class and discussed a dream about my father. I was at our summer house in Avalon, in the garden he loved. Mom was inside. Suddenly, my father appeared to me in a radiant glow. He told me that I would recover from cancer, and to try to get along with mother—even though we were so different. Then he turned into a beautiful monarch butterfly and flew away. The butterfly is the archetypal symbol of eternal life in many cultures.

Mom retired at sixty-five and lived year-round at Avalon. She enjoyed getting together with family and friends, church, civic groups, crafts, gardening and travel. Her cerebral aneurysm at the age of seventy-nine changed everything.

She lapsed into a coma following emergency surgery. The doctors were pessimistic about her recovery. Standing at Mom's bedside in the critical care unit, thinking she was dying and remembering stories of the comforting white light many people saw in that limbo world between life and death, I tried to help my mother by shouting, "Mom, can you see the light? Go toward the light!"

Mom remained in a coma for several weeks. We didn't know whether to pray for her to live or die, because the doctors said that if she came out of the coma, she might be severely brain damaged. One day, a good friend was praying over her and said loudly, "Jo, wake up and come back to us." Mom suddenly opened her eyes and gave him a big smile! She looked around the room, saw a rose in a vase by her bed, and said "beautiful"—her first word since going into the coma. The doctors called her "The Miracle Lady" and we were thrilled.

Soon, however, a CT scan revealed fluid buildup in her brain, which could cause her death. The only hope was a risky operation to help the flow of fluid from the brain and through the body. She might die during surgery, but we knew Mom would want to take the chance.

"We almost lost her," the surgeon said after the operation. My husband and I were there when Mom opened her eyes.

Looking directly at me, she asked, "Where is my mother?"

"Grandmom died a long time ago," I replied, feeling dismayed.

"But she was standing here at the foot of my bed, with her arm out toward me and a beautiful garden behind her. She wanted me to go with her."

I was stunned that my usually skeptical mother had just had a near-death experience. "What did you say to her?" I asked.

"I told her I didn't want to go with her yet—that I wanted to return to life—that she could come back for me when it was my time."

Her recovery was swift, amazing the doctors. She returned to her own home with a new belief in miracles. Not only did she heal in body, but in spirit. Mom and I became closer than ever, with a new sense of connection. I felt that my father's request in the dream had been fulfilled.

It was a special day when she took my arm

and walked to the altar of her church and read a prayer she had written, thanking the people for their visits and prayers, ending with the words: "May I be a constant reminder to everyone that God still performs miracles."

In her seven remaining years, Mom was blessed by the birth of two great-grandchildren. She also enjoyed the "little things" in life more than ever—watching the birds at her window feeder, gazing in wonder at the sunset, and connecting with God and nature on a deeper level. Sometimes we just sat together quietly, holding hands and looking at the ocean.

One night, on the evening of the full moon, I tried to call Mom at our usual time, but there was no answer. I tried again when I got to the YMCA to teach my yoga class. Still no answer. I phoned my husband and asked him to call to be sure she was all right.

At the end of each yoga class, there is a period of meditation. As my students and I sat in our circle, I prayed for Mom. Suddenly, I felt her spirit within me—joyfully letting me know that she was passing on to that other place! I drove home in a daze. I knew what had happened.

My husband met me at the door. "Honey, I'm so sorry, but we lost her. I called twice and finally got her on the phone. She had fallen and was too weak to get up. I told her to hang up and that I'd call the rescue squad right away. She wasn't in pain and didn't sound frightened. The police called a few minutes later and told me that they were talking to her as they came in the door, and then she just stopped responding. When they reached her, she was gone. She died at 7:45."

That was exactly the time I was praying and felt her spirit move through me. I know in my heart that as the rescue team came through Mom's front door, my grandmother appeared to her again. This time, Mom decided to take my grandmother's hand and go with her.

—Linda Texter Hall—

Dad's Quarters

All that is in heaven... is also on earth.
~Plotinus

My dad always collected quarters. He was delighted when the new U.S. state quarters were announced. He would go to his longtime neighborhood banker and make sure they put at least twenty rolls of each new quarter aside for him. It was a special treat and a family tradition to get your quarters from Grandpa. He gave them to his children, to his grandchildren and closest friends. He loved the whole process of collecting—carefully placing one of each state quarter in the special collectors edition portfolio as they were issued.

When my dad passed, I felt such a sense of emptiness. My father and I had been so close, I was lost without his guidance, support and wisdom. I wondered if I would ever feel my dad around me again. I wished I could have some kind of reassurance that he was there, watching over me. It was right after Hurricane Katrina and I was doing a motivational seminar for about three hundred volunteers. At the end of the event, everyone was in a circle and as I looked at the faces of these generous, committed individuals — I felt so grateful and appreciative. I again wished my dad were there to see me with these amazing people. I looked down in the center of the circle. To my astonishment, I saw nothing on the floor except for one state quarter, from North Carolina, the state in which my dad was born and raised.

Then, two months later, I went back to North Carolina to visit my mom. While I was there, I went to the bank to cash a check. The bank manager, who had known me since I was a little girl, called me into her office. The quarters for all the states my dad had ordered were in the corner of the office. She didn't know why, but she felt she needed to hold them for me.

Ever since that time, throughout the years, I have found quarters at the most extraordinary times, when I needed support the most. When I needed the strength to pull my son's tooth (a job that my dad used to be responsible for), a quarter miraculously appeared. When I need emotional support during a tough time, a quarter will show up in a strange place.

It has now become a tradition in our house and family. Every time a quarter appears, one of my kids says, "Oh, it's Grandpa!" At the most unbelievable times—even in foreign countries—a quarter appears. I found an American quarter in Fiji! Even in my brand new car—when I picked it up from the dealership, I found a quarter under the mat.

My daughter, my two sons, my mom, my friends, and I all feel a sense of peace and comfort every time a lone quarter turns up in an unexpected place. We have all accepted it as a message of love, guidance and support from my dad—and every new quarter we find makes us smile.

—Loren Slocum—

A Great Grandma Forever

*A grandmother is a little bit parent, a little bit
teacher, and a little bit best friend.*
~Author Unknown

There was nothing better than spending the night with my great-grandma Mead on New Year's Eve. I'm not sure who was more excited about the annual sleepover. Even though she was in her eighties, Grandma loved being around kids. My brother and I stayed up later than usual, playing card games for hours after we had eaten homemade fried chicken, mashed potatoes with milk gravy, bowls of fruit, and gingersnap cookies that Grandma stored in the cupboard behind her tiny kitchen table. She never allowed us to drink soda because she didn't want our teeth to decay. She was my great-grandma, but I always referred to her as Grandma.

Our eyes were wide as saucers when she told us the story of *The Three Little Pigs*. We begged her to tell the tale, and I loved hearing her say, "Not by the hair on my chinny chin chin." She loved to watch repeats of *The Lawrence Welk Show* on PBS, and she did so as she instructed us to take a shower or at the very least, wash our feet. We ate grapefruit (we never had this at our house) and toast the next morning before my mom came to pick us up. It was the best way to start the New Year. After each visit she hugged us goodbye and said, "God bless you." Then tears welled up in her eyes.

Grandma had endured tremendous loss during her life: her oldest child died in a tragic fire, her left hand was amputated after it became infected, and her husband died at an early age. She never made excuses. She raised four children by herself, including one with significant hearing loss, during the Great Depression. She earned money by cleaning houses and helping others with their children. She was proud and never received financial assistance.

A plaque hanging in her kitchen said, "Today is the day the Lord has made; let us rejoice and be glad in it." She never shared how much she leaned on her faith or how she made the conscious choice to be positive each day. Grandma fed the birds and admired the red poppies in her yard. When she gave thanks for God's gifts, she said, "Wonderful, wonderful." Her response was the same when we told her about our accomplishments. She said the same thing when she looked at a sunset or when family appeared at her door.

She passed away a few days after my husband and I returned from our honeymoon. I felt as though she had been waiting for us. At ninety-nine years old, she had her positive attitude, her mind, and her teeth. (She was proud of having her own teeth. She wanted us to have our own teeth, too, which is why she didn't allow us to drink soda.) It was hard to believe she was gone.

After Grandma's passing, my parents' doorbell began ringing at odd times. On more than one occasion, my mom sprang out of bed in a panic, wondering who might be at the door. Nobody was ever there. We decided it was Grandma saying hello.

The day my husband and I learned we were expecting twins, we laughed. On the drive home from the doctor's office, I realized it was Grandma Mead's birthday. I felt it was a sign she was there with me. The twins were born exactly six months later and were very difficult babies. They seemed to cry often and were not easily settled. They seldom slept. Two years later they both received an autism diagnosis, which explained some of their difficult behaviors. I missed her and wished she could meet my boys. It was a demanding full-time job caring for the twins. Sometimes I spoke to her aloud. I hoped she was guiding me.

When the twins were three and a half years old, my son Henry was born. He was quite vocal at an early age, which was music to my ears since my twins were receiving speech therapy. Isaac didn't speak at all, while Noah repeated words again and again. Henry, on the other hand, was speaking in full sentences before he was two years old. He loved to talk.

One afternoon, after Henry's nap, he was sitting at the table eating a snack. "Grandma Mead played with me today," he stated, matter-of-factly. I tried not to act surprised because I wanted him to tell me more about the experience. I had talked to him about Grandma Mead, but he only knew she was a special grandma.

"What happened?" I asked. "Was she in your room?"

"She told me stories," he said, as he took a few bites of his banana.

"Was it *The Three Little Pigs*?" I asked.

"No," he said. The conversation was over.

I had read about children having the ability to see those who had passed. Could Henry have interacted with Grandma Mead? Over the course of several months, he consistently reported her visits when he was in his room for a nap.

One afternoon he said to me, "Grandma Mead likes to ring doorbells."

"Yes," I answered, a bit in shock. "She likes to ring doorbells. What else did she say?"

"She lives in a house."

"Henry, she lives in heaven now, but she used to live in a house," I explained.

"Her house is red and white," he said.

I almost fell off my chair. He couldn't have possibly known any of that information. The red and white house was the one where my brother and I stayed each New Year's Eve.

When Henry was two and a half years old, he and I were outside one summer morning while the twins were at preschool. I was watching him toddle around our back patio area. As he was running, his sneaker hit an uneven patch of cement. I was too far away and knew I wouldn't be able to get there in time. I felt helpless.

As he was falling forward, he shouted, "Grandma Mead!" I was surprised by his exclamation. He landed face down on the cement. I remember thinking his injuries could be pretty severe because he hadn't put his arms out to brace his fall. I felt sick to my stomach. I picked him up and held him as he cried. I expected his shirt to be torn or his face to be bloody. I took him inside and tried to calm him down while I examined him. He didn't have a scratch on his body anywhere! It appeared as though someone had cushioned his fall.

I rocked with Henry in the glider for a long time while tears ran down my cheeks. I looked down at my little boy, nestled in my protective arms. Wonderful, wonderful, I thought. Thank you, Grandma Mead, for keeping him safe. I imagined her putting her arms around me and whispering, "God bless you."

—Tyann Sheldon Rouw—

Love Beyond the Natural

Mother, the ribbons of your love
are woven around my heart.
~Author Unknown

After the death of my stepfather, I thought it was best that my mother move in with me. Mom and I were not only mother and daughter, but also best friends. Her moving in with me at that time turned out to be the best thing for the both of us.

Mom cooked and kept the house while I worked and paid the bills. We had a system and a relationship that others envied. We went to bingo together. We went on vacations together. Her friends were mine and mine were hers. We laughed and talked. We argued and fussed. She spoiled me and I spoiled her more.

When Mom was diagnosed with cancerous brain tumors, I was told that she had approximately six months left. I was in denial and I decided that my mother's strength and determination would make her an exception to the rule; she would live forever.

Then one morning, I walked into Mom's room and found that she had passed away during the night. We didn't get a chance to hug or say goodbye. I indignantly questioned why she simply and suddenly slipped away. After doing everything together, why didn't we have the chance to fight death together? I was devastated and angry that she died alone. If only I had known that it would be her last night on earth, I never would have left her side. I questioned everything, including my worth as a daughter, a caretaker and a friend.

As time marched on, I longed for a sense of

peace and closure, but they eluded me. I needed to hear from my mother that she was okay and that I had not let her down. Depression set in and I lost interest in everything, including my pride and joy—my aquarium. Mom had often mentioned how much she enjoyed it, how beautiful it was and how well I took care of it. Now that she was gone, my attentiveness to my hobby had gone also.

Nine months passed and Mother's Day rolled around. My grieving intensified. As I dressed for church, wanting to have something of my mother's with me, I decided at the last minute to use one of her pocketbooks. I sorted through them, looking for the one that best matched my outfit, and saw the simple black one that she often carried. "Just perfect," I caught myself saying out loud. Whenever Mom had a pocketbook dilemma, she always chose that one. I was running late so I hurriedly emptied out my pocketbook, threw my stuff in along with hers and left.

I sat in church and envied the children, young and old, sitting with their mothers. I thought about the last Mother's Day I spent with Mom. As tears streamed down my face, I smiled as I remembered working in my aquarium and her asking what I wanted for Mother's Day. Without stopping or looking up, I nonchalantly said that I wanted more fish. I knew she wasn't going to get them and I really didn't want her to get me anything. I didn't need a thing, and just having a mom like her with me was the best gift of all. However, Mom bought me a beautiful pantsuit, which I loved. And as trivial as this might sound, I wondered why she hadn't given me a card. She always gave the most beautiful, heartwarming cards, and I always looked forward to receiving them. Not wanting to seem ungrateful over something so minor, I figured she just forgot, and I never mentioned anything about it.

When it was time to give the offerings, the pastor said his usual, "Give and it shall be given, ask and believe, and you will receive." I took out my offering and silently asked for something, anything from my mother. Then, thinking what a ridiculous request that was, I walked up, put my offering in the basket and sat back down.

Later that night, as I emptied my stuff from my mother's pocketbook to put back into mine, I noticed a white envelope that had my name on it. Inside was a card. On the front it read, "For my daughter, may the Lord bless you always." When I opened the card, a fifty-dollar bill fell out. I picked up the money and read the inside of the card. On the left side she wrote, "Wishing a wonderful daughter a happy Mother's Day. Here's a little something towards your fish. Wish it was more. I appreciate all you do. I love you today and I'll love you always, Mom." On the right side it simply says, "I thank the Lord so often for giving me a loving daughter I'm so proud of."

Mom always dated her cards and May 2007

was in the upper right hand corner of the card. My mother had passed away in September 2006. Was this all just a mere coincidence with a mistaken date? I don't think so. To me, it was my mother's way of telling me she was in heaven. I finally had the peace and closure I needed. As tears streamed down my face, I looked up and whispered, "I'll always love you too, Mom."

Yes, I had lost interest in my aquarium. The few fish left and the condition of the tank reflected it. I took the fifty dollars and, adding to it, I bought what I needed for the health and welfare of my old fish. And of course, I bought new fish.

Even in death, Mom's motherly love saw to my needs. That card played an essential part in getting my life and my aquarium back in order, and both were beneficial and therapeutic towards my healing. But it was the card's wording and the "I love you today and I'll love you always" that was vital. I knew her love would always be with me. True love is an eternal, mystical force that can and will go beyond the natural. For the last time, my mother left something tangible to always remind me.

—Francine L. Baldwin-Billingslea—

Meet Our Contributors

Francine L. Baldwin-Billingslea has been published in over twenty anthologies and magazines, including several in the *Chicken Soup for the Soul* series, *Whispering Angel* books, *Thin Threads*, *BellaOnline Literary Review*, and *The Rambler*, as well as authoring an inspirational memoir titled *Through It All and Out On The Other Side*.

Lisa Shearer Cooper graduated from the University of Colorado with a B.A. degree in English and M.A. degree in Education. After teaching ESL to adults for many years and authoring textbooks, she is currently engaged in memoir writing and teaching preschool. Lisa enjoys travel, hiking, gardening and yoga. E-mail her at lisa@sc3.net.

Diana Creel Elarde, BA, MA., consults and also teaches psychology for Maricopa Community College. Her husband Vincent edits and encourages her quest to become a successful writer. Amanda and Zdravko, her children, are her great sources of inspiration. E-mail her at dcgwest@live.com.

Linda Texter Hall attended Temple University and Bread Loaf Writers' Conference at Middlebury College. Her career includes seventeen years at Winterthur Museum. She is a yoga and meditation instructor, and a founding board member of Cancer Support Community Delaware. Linda enjoys creative writing and exploring "inner space."

Karen McBride has lived in the Tampa Bay area for twenty-five years, raising her three children. She enjoys exploring beautiful nature parks, photographing wildlife, and going to craft shows. She has written numerous articles for a local newspaper and has written her first children's book. E-mail her at kmcbride320@aol.com.

Dr. Barbara Poremba is a Nurse Practitioner and Professor of Nursing at Salem State University, MA. She earned degrees from Harvard University, Boston University and the University of Massachusetts Amherst and Worcester. Barbara enjoys international humanitarian work, photography, skiing, tap dancing, sea glass collecting and grandchildren. Learn more at www.salemstate.edu/~bporemba/.

Tyann Sheldon Rouw lives in Iowa with her husband and three sons. She is a previous contributor to the *Chicken Soup for the Soul* series. Visit her blog, Turn Up the Valium, at tyannsheldonrouw.weebly.com or follow her on Twitter @TyannRouw.

Jane Self is a freelance writer and copywriter. She retired as Features Editor from *The Tuscaloosa News* in 2007 after eight years and was previously Assistant Features Editor for the *Macon Telegraph* for twelve years. E-mail her at jane@janeself.com.

Loren Slocum, mother of three, International Personal Development Speaker and Elite Lifestyle Coach, "daddy's girl" and author of *Life Tuneups*, which appeared in *People* magazine as one of the Top 3 inspiring books of 2010. Loren has also published *No Greater Love* and *The Greatest Love*. E-mail her at lorenslocum@gmail.com.

Gary Stein co-founded an NYSE-member investment banking division. He has been a strategy advisor to dozens of entertainment firms, and was Executive Vice President of a 30-time Emmy-winning kids' TV company. Formally a Nashville songwriter, Gary recently authored the personal and candid book, *Confessions of an Unfiltered Mind*. E-mail him at gm.stein@verizon.net.

Jennifer Taylor holds degrees in creative writing and literature. She and her husband live in Wisconsin. She enjoys traveling, gardening, and dancing. Jennifer leads a writing critique group and is on the board of her local writers' guild. E-mail her at Jenniferch2000@yahoo.com.

Meet Amy Newmark

 **Amy Newmark** is the best-selling author, editor-in-chief, and publisher of the *Chicken Soup for the Soul* book series. Since 2008, she has published 150 new books, most of them national bestsellers in the U.S. and Canada, more than doubling the number of Chicken Soup for the Soul titles in print today. She is also the author of *Simply Happy*, a crash course in Chicken Soup for the Soul advice and wisdom that is filled with easy-to-implement, practical tips for having a better life.

Amy is credited with revitalizing the Chicken

Soup for the Soul brand, which has been a publishing industry phenomenon since the first book came out in 1993. By compiling inspirational and aspirational true stories curated from ordinary people who have had extraordinary experiences, Amy has kept the twenty-four-year-old Chicken Soup for the Soul brand fresh and relevant.

Amy graduated *magna cum laude* from Harvard University where she majored in Portuguese and minored in French. She then embarked on a three-decade career as a Wall Street analyst, a hedge fund manager, and a corporate executive in the technology field. She is a Chartered Financial Analyst.

Her return to literary pursuits was inevitable, as her honors thesis in college involved traveling throughout Brazil's impoverished northeast region, collecting stories from regular people. She is delighted to have come full circle in her writing career — from collecting stories "from the people" in Brazil as a twenty-year-old to, three decades later, collecting stories "from the people" for Chicken Soup for the Soul.

When Amy and her husband Bill, the CEO of Chicken Soup for the Soul, are not working, they are visiting their four grown children and their first grandchild.

Follow Amy on Twitter @amynewmark. Listen to her free podcast — "Chicken Soup for the Soul with Amy Newmark" — on Apple Podcasts, Google Play, the Podcasts app on iPhone, or by using your favorite podcast app on other devices.

Changing lives one story at a time®
www.chickensoup.com